By Gemma Barder

WAYLAND
www.waylandbooks.co.uk

PET EXPERT: RABBITS

With their twitchy noses and long, soft ears, it's no wonder rabbits are one of the world's most popular pets. Rabbits are great company and fun to look after, but there are lots of things you need to know before becoming a true Pet Expert! In this book you'll discover all about different breeds of rabbit, where the first pet rabbits came from and the best way to care for your bunny. When you've finished reading, there's an exciting quiz to reveal if you've truly become a Pet Expert!

CONTENTS

BUNNY BANTER

FIVE FACTS

From floppy ears to magnificent markings, get to know these popular bunny breeds a little better.

HOLLAND LOP

This floppy-eared bunny has been popular since the 1950s. With its long, floppy ears, beautiful coat and friendly personality, Holland Lops make perfect pets. However they don't like to be kept cooped up in a hutch, so make sure you give them plenty of exercise.

DID YOU KNOW?

Rabbits' teeth never stop growing. They need to nibble and chew almost constantly to keep their choppers neat and tidy.

MINI REX

The Mini Rex rabbit has a thick coat with straight, soft ears and a calm personality – which makes it the perfect pet rabbit! Mini Rex rabbits come in lots of different colours and markings and are slightly smaller than other domesticated breeds.

1.5 million

40 million

There are 1.5 million pet rabbits in the UK, and it is thought that there could be nearly 40 million in the wild!

JERSEY WOOLY

As their name suggests, these little bunnies have a soft, woolly coat. They need brushing at least once a week. These small rabbits have straight ears and a compact body. Jersey Woolies are often known as 'no-kick bunnies' as they don't often kick out or bite.

DUTCH RABBIT

You can easily spot a Dutch rabbit by their distinctive colour patterns. Despite their name, they were actually developed in the UK and were the most popular breed of rabbit for a long time before smaller breeds of rabbit were introduced. They make clever and playful pets.

DID YOU KNOW?

A female rabbit is called a doe and a male rabbit is called a buck.

REMARKABLE RABBITS

From the smallest to the most mysterious, take a look at these super-rare rabbits.

DID YOU KNOW?

A species called the Sumatran Striped rabbit is so rare that it has only been photographed a few times!

COLUMBIA BASIN PYGMY RABBIT

These teeny bunnies are the world's smallest breed of rabbit. They only weigh around 450 grams when fully grown and are about the same size as a kitten! In the wild, they live in a small area of Washington State in the USA and were almost extinct in the 1990s.

SOUTHEAST ASIAN STRIPED RABBIT

This unusual rabbit was discovered 20 years ago in the remote Annamite Mountains of Laos and Vietnam – and sightings have been rare ever since. Its fur is light brown with dark brown stripes and it has short ears. It can grow to around 40 cm long, but there is still lots more to learn about this mysterious bunny!

TEDDYWIDDER

Is that a rabbit or a big pom-pom? Teddywidders come from the Netherlands, Germany and Belgium and have fur that grows over 5 cm long. Teddywidders have floppy (or lop) ears, which makes them slightly different to their Teddy Dwerg cousins who have pointy ears.

In 1998 there were only 16 Columbia Basin Pygmy rabbits, while the number of pet rabbits in the US is 2.2 million!

VOLCANO RABBIT

The Volcano rabbit lives in mountainous areas of Mexico. They are very hard to spot and in some areas have been declared extinct. The destruction of their natural habitat, together with global warming, has forced this bunny breed to make its home higher up the mountains. Volcano rabbits are the second smallest rabbit breed in the world and have short, fluffy ears.

DID YOU KNOW?

The Volcano rabbit lets out a high-pitched squeak when it thinks it is in danger, rather than thumping its feet like other breeds.

BUNNY BANTER

Rabbits have a secret language to tell you (and other rabbits) how they are feeling. Find out exactly what it means when your bunny hops, thumps and twitches.

EARS

As different breeds have different types of ears (straight, floppy, small) it can be hard to tell what they are doing with them. A little shake followed by jumping shows playfulness and excitement. Ears pricked up means they are feeling cautious about what is going on around them.

STANDING

If your rabbit is standing on its hind legs, it could be trying to get a better view of something, or simply begging for more food! If they are standing on all fours, they are getting ready to see what's coming next.

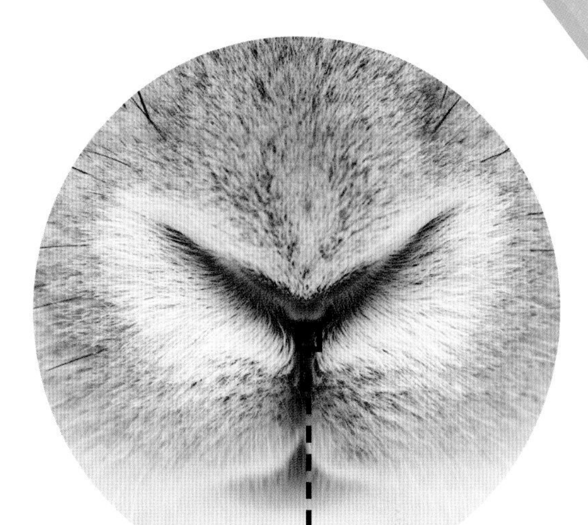

NOSES

Rabbits use their noses as a way of communicating how they feel. Frantic twitching can indicate that they are excited or anxious. Nose rubbing is a sign of affection, while nose bumping can mean they want attention (or for you to move out the way!).

LEGS

One of the most common things rabbits do with their back legs is thump. In most cases this means they are scared or unhappy about something. If they are lying with their legs in the air or flat out behind them, you have one happy bunny!

KITS

These cute little bundles don't take long to grow up! Read all about baby bunnies – called kits – before they hop away!

EARLY DAYS

When kits are born they are blind and furless. They live snuggled up to their brothers and sisters in a fur-lined nest until they can see and their fur grows. Unlike a bird's nest, mother rabbits don't actually sit on this nest and will leave the kits for long periods of time.

DID YOU KNOW?

The average number of kits in a litter is 8-9. The world record for kits in a litter is 24!

TIME TO GROW

A baby rabbit should stay with its mother until it is at least eight weeks old. Kits become adult rabbits at around six months old, which is when they can start to have kits of their own!

DID YOU KNOW?

It's possible for a female rabbit to have around 800 children, grandchildren and great grandchildren in one year.

30 days

660 days

Rabbits are only pregnant for 30 days, while an elephant can be pregnant for 660 days!

WEANING

Newborn kits only drink their mother's milk. After two weeks they will start to eat other foods, such as hay and carrots to begin with, before moving on to more adventurous foods.

BUNNY LOVE!

Discover everything you need to know about keeping your bunny happy, healthy and well fed!

FOOD AND DRINK

Rabbits need a fresh supply of hay at all times. Bunnies like to graze, rather than eating lots all in one go, so snacking between meals is definitely OK! They like fresh vegetables and rabbit pellets, which give them lots of fibre. They also need fresh water throughout the day in a bowl or bottle.

GROOMING

Rabbits like to keep themselves clean, but that doesn't mean you can leave them to look after themselves completely. Long-haired rabbits will need brushing at least once a week to stop their fur from matting and all rabbits need their nails trimmed regularly.

FUN WITH FRIENDS

A happy rabbit is a rabbit with friends. Rabbits need to be kept with at least one other bunny and they like to see you, too! Spend time with your rabbit at least twice a day.

HEATSTROKE

If your bunny is outside on a hot day, keep an eye out for heatstroke symptoms, which include; red ears, dribbling, moving slowly and sometimes convulsions.

BUNNY PROOFING

If you are planning to exercise your rabbit indoors, you'll need to do some bunny proofing first! Make sure all wires are tied up out of reach or covered in plastic tubing. Put plastic guards on your skirting boards, too.

HEALTH

Bunnies can get poorly, so it is a good idea to keep an eye on how they behave. If your rabbit is eating less or having trouble pooing, it could be a sign of illness. Keep an eye out for an extra-scratchy bunny as it could have fleas!

PLAY TIME

When you play with your rabbit, come down to their level and play on the floor as rabbits don't like to be high up. Make a 'castle' out of old cardboard boxes for them to explore and chew.

DID YOU KNOW?

Rabbits and guinea pigs do not get on! They don't understand each other and can get into fights.

FACTFILE

TOYS!

Rabbits love to play with toys like these:

- a cardboard tube stuffed with hay
- baby toys (non-electronic)
- straw hats
- tunnels.

RABBIT RULES

Read the Pet Expert guide on the dos and don'ts of bunny care.

DO:

keep rabbits in pairs or in threes as they love company.

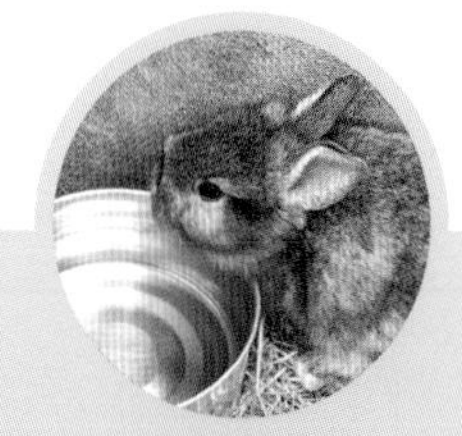

provide two water bowls or bottles if you are away for more than a few hours.

buy good quality food and hay.

get your bunnies vaccinated. Your vet will tell you which vaccinations they need.

research the right type of rabbit for you.

brush them regularly.

keep vegetable peelings to add to their diet.

play with them often.

DON'T:

keep them in a hutch or run that is too small.

keep them outside when it is very cold.

play with or stroke them when they are anxious. Leave them to calm down.

keep them in a cage with a wire floor as it is bad for their feet.

give them toys that they could get stuck in, such as a hamster ball.

forget to clean out their hutch.

FOOD FOR RABBITS

✔	✘
carrot tops	chocolate
bok choy	fried food
celery	avocado
coriander	apple seeds
clover	bread
basil	onion

RABBIT HABITAT

There's lots to consider when you begin to create the perfect palace for your rabbit friends. Get started by reading these hints and tips.

INDOORS OR OUTDOORS?

It can be confusing to decide whether your rabbit should live indoors or outdoors. Talk to the breeder to see how your bunnies have been living before they come to you and consider talking to your vet. Always remember to bring your rabbit indoors if the weather is very cold or hot.

FACTFILE

The Pet Expert guide to hutch size!

- It should be tall enough for your bunny to sit up straight on its back legs.
- It should be wide enough for your adult-sized bunny to hop twice.
- It should be long enough for your adult-sized bunny to hop three times.
- Attach a run to your hutch so your bunny gets plenty of exercise.

HAPPIEST HUTCH

A hutch should have a place for sleeping and a place for looking out. Most hutches have a dark 'hidey hole' as well as a section covered in mesh or wire for your bunny to look out of.

DID YOU KNOW?

You should never buy a hutch or cage with a wire floor. Wire floors can be painful for rabbits to walk on and give them injuries.

GETTING READY

Before you introduce your rabbit to their new home, it's time to make it nice and cosy! Start by lining the bottom of your cage with newspaper, then top with wood shavings (not cedar or pine as these can be toxic). Line the sleeping area of your hutch with soft hay, too.

FACTFILE

Where to place your outdoors hutch:

- Choose a spot that is close to the house.
- A shady spot is a great choice for warmer weather.
- Be aware of any plants that might overhang - make sure they aren't toxic to hungry bunnies.
- Make sure the hutch is away from any other animals.

DID YOU KNOW?

Any plant that is grown from a bulb is toxic to rabbits. This includes daffodils and tulips!

THE HISTORY OF RABBITS

From the Spanish wilderness to your back garden, bunnies have a very interesting history.

3000 BCE

LAND OF THE RABBITS!

One theory about how Spain got its name dates back to around 2,300 years ago. The theory goes that the ancient Romans called it 'Hispania', a word that came from another ancient language – Phonenican – and means 'Land of the rabbits'.

220 BCE

ROMANS

The ancient Romans knew how important rabbits were for providing food to eat and warm clothing to wear. Although the Romans built giant rabbit farms, the rabbits were notorious for tunnelling to freedom.

CE 40

ACROSS THE OCEANS

As the ancient Romans travelled across the globe, so did their rabbits! Romans would take the rabbits on voyages for food and breed them in each new country they settled in. As always, many rabbits escaped and found new homes in the fields and countryside.

TODAY

Rabbits are the third most popular pet in the world after cats and dogs. There are now over 200 breeds worldwide.

CE 600

MONKS

From CE 600, there are records of rabbits being kept in monasteries, where monks lived and worked. Although the rabbits were still used for food and clothing, the monks took pride in caring for them, and began to breed varieties with different coats and markings.

1900s

VICTORIANS

Life changed for some rabbits in the 1900s. As well as being hunted and kept for food, the Victorians could see that rabbits had other charms. It became fashionable to attend rabbit competitions, where owners would compete to see who had the best bunny. Rabbits also began to be kept as pets for lucky boys and girls.

1939

WORLD WAR

During the Second World War (1939–45), the British government encouraged people to keep rabbits to help feed families during rationing – a time when food was limited. After the war ended, many people kept their rabbits as pets.

BUNNY STARS

There have been some legendary rabbits in books and on screen. How much do you know about these bunny superstars?

BUGS BUNNY

Everyone has heard of Bugs Bunny. The wise-cracking rabbit has been around for nearly 90 years and has his own star on the Hollywood Walk of Fame. His first appearance was in a short animated film that was nominated for an Oscar!

DID YOU KNOW?

Mel Blanc (the voice behind Bugs Bunny) munched on real carrots while recording the character.

PETER RABBIT

When Beatrix Potter first wrote *The Tale of Peter Rabbit*, her publishers didn't think it would be much of a success. Today the little book has sold over 40 million copies and has been translated into 35 different languages! It has also been turned into a TV series and a blockbuster film.

THE WHITE RABBIT

If it wasn't for this little bunny's waistcoat, Alice may never have followed him and fallen down the rabbit hole into Wonderland! Written in 1865 by Lewis Carroll, *Alice's Adventures in Wonderland* has made The White Rabbit almost as famous as The Mad Hatter or Alice herself.

DID YOU KNOW?

Alice's Adventures in Wonderland has been translated into 174 different languages!

MIFFY

This cute little pure-white rabbit was created by Dutch artist, Dick Bruna, in the 1950s and she is still popular today. Miffy has featured in nearly 30 books that have sold 45 million copies all over the world and she can be found on everything from pyjamas to lunchboxes.

DID YOU KNOW?

Miffy's birthday is 21st June and she is over 60 years old!

BRILLIANT BUNNIES

These rabbits are the biggest, longest and furriest bunnies around. Read on to discover their amazing achievements!

2 cm

76 cm

At only 2 cm tall, the world's smallest breed of bunny is the Netherlands Dwarf. The average Flemish Giant rabbit grows to 76 cm!

Nipper's Geronimo was an English Lop just like this one!

LONGEST EARS

The longest ears of any rabbit belonged to Nipper's Geronimo, an English Lop rabbit whose ears measured 79 cm long!

OLD-TIMER

The oldest-known rabbit lived to be 18 years and 10 months old. He was a wild rabbit, caught in Tasmania, Australia in 1964 and was named Flopsy.

GIANT BUNNY

Darius is a Flemish Giant rabbit, just like this one. He has been recognised as the world's longest rabbit at 129 cm, which makes him about the same size as a small dog. Although they look hard to handle, Flemish Giants are easy to look after as they are so chilled out!

MORE AMAZING BUNNY FACTS!

- The oldest living rabbit is a bunny called Hazel, who is 16 years old (that's more than twice the average life expectancy).
- The biggest rabbit jump ever recorded is 99.5 cm by a bunny called Mimrelunds Tösen from Denmark!

HAIR-RAISING

Franchesca the English Angora rabbit not only has beautiful fur, she has record-breaking fur! At 36.5 cm long, Franchesca has the longest rabbit fur in the world and is often mistaken for a Pekinese dog!

Angora rabbits like this one need regular brushing or their fur can get matted.

DID YOU KNOW?

Angora rabbits can make loveable pets. They are intelligent and love to play with their owners.

FIVE FACTS

Take a look at these amazing (and sometimes gross) facts about our brilliant bunny friends.

1 THEY EAT THEIR OWN POO!

Weird, but true! Rabbits make two types of poo: a soft black ball and a hard pellet. By eating the soft poo, the rabbit can get even more nutrients out of their food.

2 THEY SLEEP WITH THEIR EYES OPEN.

Rabbits can fall asleep while their eyes are still on the lookout for predators.

THEY AREN'T RODENTS.

Instead, rabbits come from the Leporidae family, which also includes hares.

THEY CAN'T BE SICK.

Rabbits don't have the ability to throw up, so it's vital that you feed your pet rabbit the right food to keep their tummies healthy.

THEY ARE CREPUSCULAR.

This is just a fancy way of saying that they are most active in the morning and early evening.

YOUR BEST BUNNY

Can we match your personality to your dream pet? Answer the questions and follow the flow to find out!

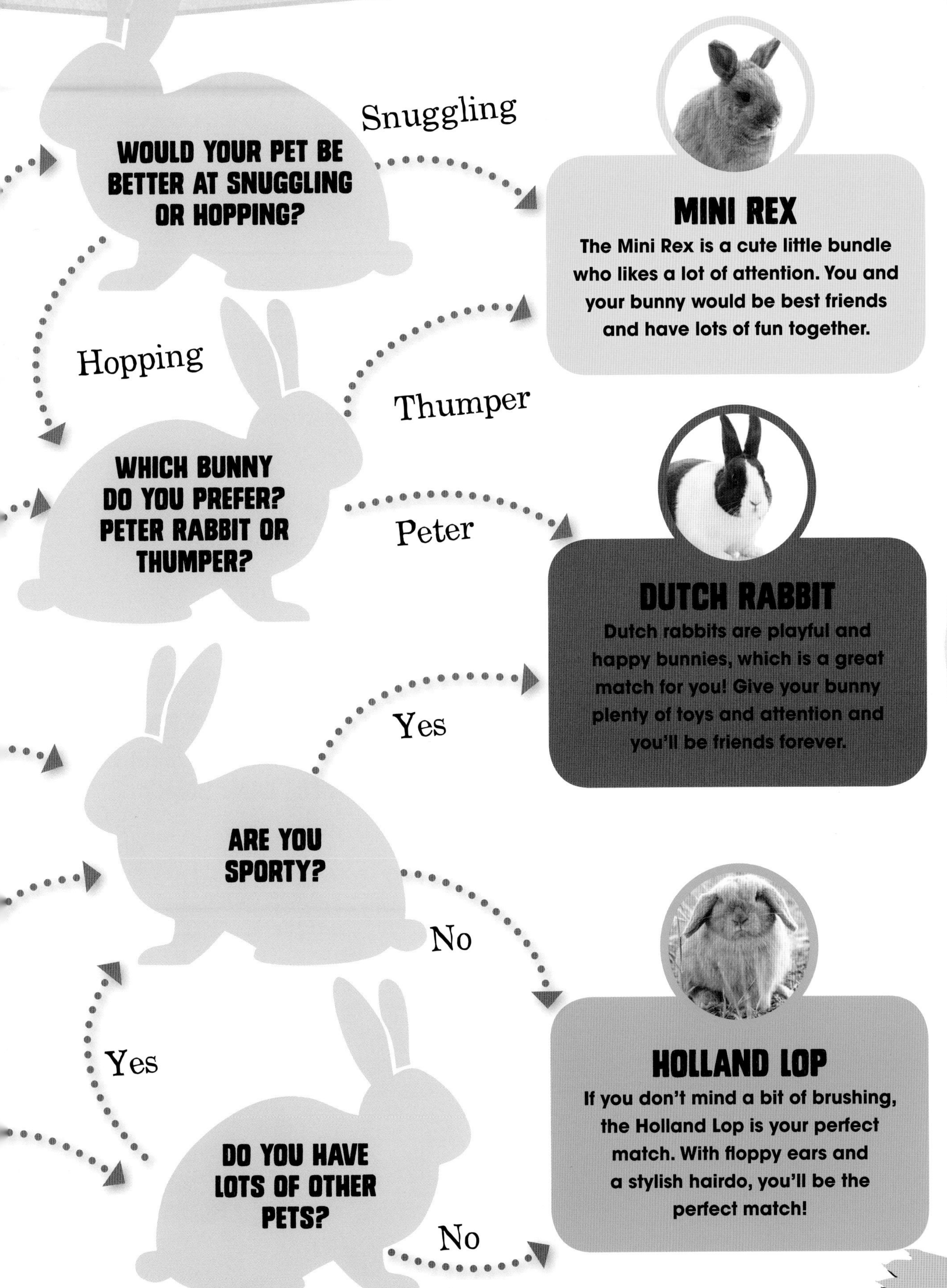

MINI REX

The Mini Rex is a cute little bundle who likes a lot of attention. You and your bunny would be best friends and have lots of fun together.

DUTCH RABBIT

Dutch rabbits are playful and happy bunnies, which is a great match for you! Give your bunny plenty of toys and attention and you'll be friends forever.

HOLLAND LOP

If you don't mind a bit of brushing, the Holland Lop is your perfect match. With floppy ears and a stylish hairdo, you'll be the perfect match!

Now you've read all about rabbits, do you think you are a Pet Expert? Take the quiz to find out!

WHAT IS A FEMALE BUNNY CALLED?

a) a flo
b) a doe
c) a bow

HOW BIG IS A FULLY-GROWN COLUMBIA BASIN PYGMY RABBIT?

a) the same size as a kitten
b) the same size as a parrot
c) the same size as a mouse

HOW MANY TYPES OF POO DO RABBITS MAKE?

a) one
b) two
c) three

HOW LONG ARE RABBITS PREGNANT FOR?

a) 30 days
b) 60 days
c) 90 days

WHY SHOULDN'T YOU KEEP RABBITS AND GUINEA PIGS IN THE SAME HOME?

a) they fight
b) they don't understand each other
c) both

The answers can be found on page 30.

WHICH FOOD SHOULD RABBITS AVOID?

a) celery
b) clover
c) avocado

WHAT TYPE OF FLOOR IS HARMFUL TO BUNNIES?

a) marble
b) wire
c) wood

HOW MANY BREEDS OF RABBIT ARE THERE?

a) 20
b) 200
c) 2000

9

WHO WROTE *THE TALE OF PETER RABBIT*?

a) Enid Blyton
b) C.S. Lewis
c) Beatrix Potter

WHAT TYPE OF RABBIT HAS THE LONGEST FUR?

a) Flemish Giant
b) Dutch rabbit
c) Angora

GLOSSARY

ANXIOUS
Feeling worried or nervous

BREED
Rabbits that share the same characteristics and physical appearance

COAT
A rabbit's fur

DOMESTICATED
To live or work alongside humans

EXTINCT
There are no more living members of that type or breed of animal

GLOBAL WARMING
Earth becoming warmer as a result of pollution in the air, which has an effect on the environment

GRAZE
To eat lightly throughout the day

HEATSTROKE
An illness caused by being exposed to too much heat

HUTCH
A rabbit's home, usually made out of wood

KITS
Baby rabbits

LEPORIDAE
A group of animals that includes hares, rabbits, and pikas (a mammal with a round body and ears, short limbs and no tail)

LOP
Rabbit ears that droop down instead of standing up straight

MATTED/MATTING
Fur or hair that is tangled into a thick lump

MONASTERY
A building kept for prayer, where monks or nuns live and work

PREGNANT
A rabbit with kits growing inside her

TOXIC
Something that is poisonous

VACCINATED
To give medicine to your pet to stop them from becoming ill

WEANING
Introducing food to a baby rabbit

QUIZ ANSWERS

1. B, 2. A, 3. B, 4. A, 5. C, 6. C, 7. B, 8. B, 9. C, 10. C.

First published in Great Britain in 2019 by Wayland

Editor: Dynamo Limited
Designer: Dynamo Limited
HB ISBN: 978 1 5263 0865 8
PB ISBN: 978 1 5263 0866 5

Printed and bound in China
Wayland, an imprint of
Hachette Children's Group
Part of Hodder and Stoughton
Carmelite House
50 Victoria Embankment
London EC4Y 0DZ
An Hachette UK Company
www.hachette.co.uk
www.hachettechildrens.co.uk

Picture acknowledgements:

All images courtesy of Getty Images iStock apart from:
Cat'chy Images/Shutterstock: front cover l, Everett Collection/Alamy:21br,
Pictorial Press Ltd/Alamy: 21c, Tierfotoagentur/Alamy: 23tr.
(Key: l - left, br - bottom right, c - centre, tr - top right)